March 10, 2003

To Kate,

Happy birthday 🎵 Keep yourself healthy and beautiful. Don't forget to pray always 🎵 Your family and I will always be here for you 🎵

I love you 🎵

Best friends always 🎵 forever lagi

kahit kailan
your best friend,
Mae Aurelia

Stories
Jesus Told

Sana, mas marami ka pa ng matutu-
nan tungkol kay Jesus. at rememb-
rance ko ito sa'yo♡

Love : mae

Louis Weber, C.E.O.
Publications International, Ltd.
7373 North Cicero Avenue
Lincolnwood, Illinois 60646

Manufactured in China.

8 7 6 5 4 3 2 1

ISBN: 0-7853-2841-6

Publications International, Ltd.

Stories Jesus Told

Written by
Etta G. Wilson

Illustrated by
Gary Torrisi

Publications International, Ltd.

When Jesus taught people, he often told special stories called parables. A parable is a make-believe story that teaches a special lesson. Jesus used these stories to explain the secrets of God's kingdom.

One day, the teachers of the town where Jesus was staying complained about Jesus. They thought he was spending too much time with people who had done bad things.

Jesus answered them by telling a parable about a man with two sons.

Many years ago, there was a man who had two sons. His sons lived with him and helped on the family farm. One day, the man's younger son decided that he did not want to help his father anymore. He asked his father for part of the family property because he wanted to leave home.

The father was very sad because he did not want his son to go. But he gave the younger son the share that was coming to him. The son packed all his belongings and left home.

The younger son traveled to a country far away. There, he spent his time going to parties and having a good time with his friends.

But the day came when all the money his father had given him was gone. He looked for his new friends to ask for help, but they were nowhere to be found.

About the same time, a terrible famine spread through the whole land. Soon he had nothing to eat.

The younger son decided to look for a job. The only work he could find was looking after pigs.

The younger son was glad to have the job. He was so hungry that he would have eaten what the pigs ate!

While he looked after the pigs, he remembered all the good things in his father's house. Finally he came to his senses. "In my father's house even the servants eat well. And here I am dying of hunger!"

The son decided to return to his father. He would ask to be forgiven and to be taken back as a servant. He set out for home. But when his father saw him coming, he ran out and hugged him and kissed him.

The son said, "Father, I have sinned against God and against you. I am no longer good enough to be called your son."

But his father called the servants and ordered a great celebration to welcome home his younger son.

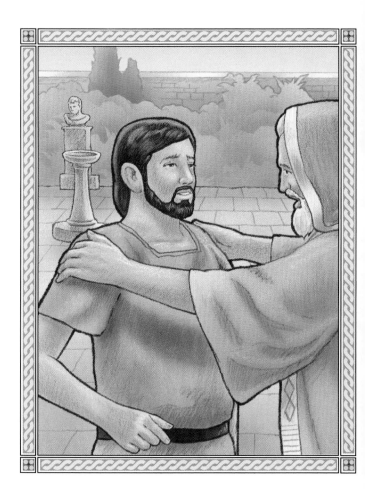

The older son was angry about the feast. He said to his father, "I have always worked for you, and you never gave me a feast!"

The father answered, "Son, you are always with me and all I have is yours. Your brother made a mistake, but he has returned. I thought he was dead, but he's alive!"

Jesus told this story to explain that God loves and accepts anyone who is sorry for the bad things that they have done.

Jesus told another story about helping people: A man was on the road from Jerusalem to Jericho. His goods were loaded on a donkey. As he walked along this road, he was attacked by thieves. They wounded the poor man and took everything he had. Then they left him lying nearly dead in the road.

A priest passed by the wounded man on the road but did not stop to help. One of the helpers in the temple also went down the road, but he did not stop to aid the man either.

Then another man from a place called Samaria came along the road.

He was a Samaritan, and many people did not like the Samaritans. But when he saw the wounded man, he felt sorry for him.

The Samaritan man washed and bandaged the injured man's wounds. Then he put the injured man on his own donkey and took him the rest of the way to Jericho.

When they arrived in Jericho, the Samaritan brought the man to an inn. He rented a room and looked after the man all night.

The next day, the Samaritan had to leave. He gave the owner of the inn some money and said, "Take care of the man I brought here. He is badly wounded. If you spend more money looking after him, I will pay you back when I return."

Jesus told this story to help us understand that we should always help people whenever we can, even if they are different from us.

If you were in trouble, you would want someone to help you. Remember this: You might need help from a stranger one day, too. How can you expect people to help you if you don't help them? Offer help whenever it's needed!

The End